Discoveries

Tim Dooley is a tutor for The Poetry School and a mentor for the prison charity, Koestler Arts. He was reviews and features editor of *Poetry London* between 2008 and 2018, a visiting lecturer at the University of Westminster from 2016 to 2021 and a judge for the John Pollard International Poetry Competition at Trinity College Dublin in 2019 and 2020. He was previously a schoolteacher for many years. His poetry collections include the Poetry Book Society Recommendations: *Tenderness* (Smith Doorstop, 2003), *Keeping Time* (Salt, 2008), and *Weemoed* (Eyewear, 2017).

Also by Two Rivers Poets

David Attwooll, *The Sound Ladder* (2015)
Charles Baudelaire, *Paris Scenes* translated by Ian Brinton (2021)
William Bedford, *The Dancers of Colbek* (2020)
Kate Behrens, *Man with Bombe Alaska* (2016)
Kate Behrens, *Penumbra* (2019)
Kate Behrens, *Transitional Spaces* (2022)
Conor Carville, *English Martyrs* (2019)
David Cooke, *A Murmuration* (2015)
David Cooke, *Sicilian Elephants* (2021)
Terry Cree, *Fruit* (2014)
Claire Dyer, *Interference Effects* (2016)
Claire Dyer, *Yield* (2021)
John Froy, *Sandpaper & Seahorses* (2018)
James Harpur, *The Examined Life* (2021)
Maria Teresa Horta, *Point of Honour* translated by Lesley Saunders (2019)
Ian House, *Nothing's Lost* (2014)
Ian House, *Just a Moment* (2020)
Rosie Jackson & Graham Burchell, *Two Girls and a Beehive* (2020)
Gill Learner, *Chill Factor* (2016)
Gill Learner, *Change* (2021)
Sue Leigh, *Chosen Hill* (2018)
Sue Leigh, *Her Orchards* (2021)
Becci Louise, *Octopus Medicine* (2017)
Mairi MacInnes, *Amazing Memories of Childhood, etc.* (2016)
Steven Matthews, *On Magnetism* (2017)
Henri Michaux, *Storms under the Skin* translated by Jane Draycott (2017)
René Noyau, *Earth on Fire and other Poems* translated by Gérard Noyau
    with Peter Pegnall (2021)
James Peake, *Reaction Time of Glass* (2019)
James Peake, *The Star in the Branches* (2022)
John Pilling & Peter Robinson (eds.), *The Rilke of Ruth Speirs:
    New Poems, Duino Elegies, Sonnets to Orpheus & Others* (2015)
Peter Robinson & David Inshaw, *Bonjour Mr Inshaw* (2020)
Lesley Saunders, *Nominy-Dominy* (2018)
Lesley Saunders, *This Thing of Blood & Love* (2022)
Jack Thacker, *Handling* (2018)
Susan Utting, *Half the Human Race* (2017)
Jean Watkins, *Precarious Lives* (2018)

Discoveries

Tim Dooley

First published in the UK in 2022 by Two Rivers Press
7 Denmark Road, Reading RG1 5PA.
www.tworiverspress.com

© Tim Dooley 2022

The right of the poet to be identified as the author of this work
has been asserted by him in accordance with the Copyright, Designs
and Patents Act of 1988.

All rights reserved. No part of this publication may be reproduced,
stored in or introduced into a retrieval system, or transmitted,
in any form, or by any means (electronic, mechanical, photocopying,
recording or otherwise) without the prior written permission
of the publisher.

ISBN 978-1-909747-98-2

1 2 3 4 5 6 7 8 9

Two Rivers Press is represented in the UK by Inpress Ltd
and distributed by Ingram Publisher Services UK.

Cover design and illustration by Sally Castle
Text design by Nadja Guggi and typeset in Janson and Parisine

Printed and bound in Great Britain by Severn, Gloucester

Acknowledgements

Some of these poems appeared previously in print or online through
the following anthologies, magazines and websites: *Acumen*, *Bad Kid
Catullus* (Sidekick Press), *Café Review*, *Envoi*, *The Fortnightly Review*,
The Honest Ulsterman, *Live Canon Anthology* 2018, *Long Poem Magazine*,
Obsessed with Pipework, *One Hand Clapping*, *Perverse*, *Poetry London*,
Poetry Scotland, *Prototype*, *Raceme*, *Stand*, *Wretched Strangers*
(Boiler House Press), *Write Where We Are Now* (MMU).

Contents

Let the dog bark | 1
Boy | 4
A Recent Year | 5
36 Views of Mont Frugy | 6
6 Panels | 8
Diving into *The Waves* | 14
Palette | 16
Room | 17
Andalucía | 18
Yellow | 19
The remixes | 20
    Fragments from the triple-gorge | 20
    Irises on Whittlesey Mere | 22
    Forest Burial | 24
Response to a Request | 25
At the Emperor's Court | 26
Legend | 27
An Old Tale | 28
Traffiques and Discoveries | 29
2020 Visions | 37
    Taking Notice | 37
    Dublin, 31.1.20 | 38
    Breaking Away | 39
    Naming the Wind | 40
    The Maze | 41
    Comrades | 42
    Distractions | 43
    Circles | 44
    Llandudno | 45
    Roses | 46
    Back from Leave | 47
    Looking Westward | 48
    The Pear Tree | 49
    There's dancing | 50

The Mysteries | 52
Mornington Crescent | 54
Defrosting | 55
Tomsk | 56
Flying out of Constantinople | 57

Let the dog bark

at the heat haze rising from the estuary
at the open-top Porsche parked on double yellow lines
at the Italian detective
at a people-facing professional
at a slug on the carpet
at a gilded elevator
at those who ride in it
at the result of the enquiry
at the mysteries of the cosmos
at the miseries of the conscious
at the surprise of a book in the mail
at the ineffable word
at the smell of paint
at paint poorly applied
at a flash of light behind blackout curtains
on sensing the perfume of a dying orange
on meeting a friend
at neuroscience
at the uncharitable in pulpits
at the middle-aged on skateboards

Let the dog whimper

Let the dog bark
as your lower body enters the scanner
as the mathematician enters the hedge fund
as the protest vigil assembles outside the clinic

Let the dog howl
at what she has seen
at what cannot be said

Let the dog bark
in all innocence
in irritation
because of the heat
for no reason
for freedom
playfully
against orders
against the will of the pack
in the middle of the afternoon
in the heart of the city
at light on an oil-spill
at the lapping of water
after licking the pavement

Let the dog bark

Let the dog bark
out of fear
from hunger
for companionship
for fancy

Let the dog lie in the sun and stretch herself
exulting in what is yet to come

Let the dog sniff
the white van's rear tyres
the stains on your jeans
the suitcase on wheels
the unseen presence
the excrement of others

Let the dog bark

Let the dog bark
for beauty
for the clicking of heels
for the burst of music
for the shock of yellow
because she does not feel disgust
because she is a dancer
because she is pleased to see you

Let the dog bark

Let her bark
after a period of silence
at the sound of thunder
as the evening comes

Let the dog bark at the moon.

Boy

his subject is the sea and he is
subject to the sea there is no
subtext his subject is the sea and
he reflects the way it varies even
as it seems so still it seems so
still there is no subtext but it is
not still it varies there is
movement here that he reflects
on and he reflects this as he
stares out from the surface where
it seems a horizontal line a little
below eye-level runs either side
of his head a clean draughtsman's
line that separates sea and sky

his mind may be working to
empty itself of what he sees to
empty itself of what has been
seen so he looks at a sea that
seems empty the sea he knows is
storied that stores what he has
seen bodies he could not look at
that looked him in the eye
companions known unknown and
not forgotten in the too-full boat
on the lonely sea that is not
empty the filled boat that rocked
him that left him rocked and
looking toward us now

A Recent Year

Everything is Art. Everything is Politics.
— Ai Weiwei

The leader is late, so we go to the café.
There is gossip about the contenders.
All of us, we want to believe in change.
The leader arrives, taller than we expected.

There's a story in Livy of a captive woman raped
by a centurion. She took her revenge: bringing
his head in her cloak to the feet of her husband.
This was somewhere near Ankara among the Galatians.

From the side it looks like the cross-section
of a landscape – say the Sussex Downs.
Or the rust-coloured ends of the rebars
could be said to resemble different types of grain.

In the first video the boy is always seen covering
his mouth with his hand. They would comment
about his breath. In the second he carries a blade
and a flag. His voice is loud and unforgiving.

Desperate people are still fleeing from desperate situations.
Bad choices have undoubtedly been made
We're told *this* is the marginal, says the stranger.
The gallery is silent; the visitors shockingly still.

36 Views of Mont Frugy

At 87 metres a climb might not be a sufficient challenge.
We took the long view, assembling across the river
south of the market, facing the Resistance park where
the plaque says Charles De Gaulle made his final speech.

We thought a height of fifty would do it (for our human
pyramid), but a look at the maths lit up the exponential
support requirements needed for shouldering the affair.
2,500 to be gathered through the influence of networks.

Imagine the view from the heart of our man-and-woman-
mountain, the middle of row twenty-five, with twenty-five
bodies on either side, some eighteen hundred below and
six-fifty, I think, queuing by the cherry-pickers. Dizzying

in conception, it faltered on the news that no pyramid had
been made more than nine bodies high. So we took this more
circumspect route up and round between bushes and under
the leaves of ever-overhanging trees. Had I a good hand,

I would picture for you effects of shade on varied yellows
ambers, greens, the aching-arced ellipsis of the avenue
bursting suddenly to an open blue and honeyed light as
the leafmeal crumbled steadily under our heels. Better

though to reach into the facts of the thing, the original
site of the city where the Steir and Odet meet, a sort of
granite cliff, left to pig-grazing once the valley was made
safe, planted with beech and sessile oak. Trees uprooted

thirty years ago in the great storm are growing back, but
erosion made worse by traffic and high-rise building make
falling rocks a safety issue. Or would you rather hear how
in the bardic days Riwal brought Cerialtan here offering

him all the land he could see if he betrayed his ward, the silver-footed boy. Imagine yourself taken to a high place now and seeing the river that trickles through the town widen, separate and join itself again journeying to the sea.

Or from higher, lifted as in a balloon drifting over the town, look back at the hill framed by the life around it. A group are flying a kite and some workers are repairing the red tiles of a roof – and 'Be careful' you want to cry, 'Don't slip!'

6 Panels

(after Anni Albers)

1

From the 3rd floor balcony
a   striped sky   plays
its unifying   blue notes
imagine *a tree*   crafted
from *brown copper*   un-
insulated wire   *woven
into branches* from which
silver leaves seem to hang
as   if   contributing a
thought   imagine also
each twig's commitment
to its orchestration may
birds *waken in you*   when
the angry clouds   have
moved on   take up the
hammer then if you must
it is time   to   fashion
a shield   with the *tensile
strength* of a spider's web

2

Fragile in the light wind
a bridge holds its line and
the weight of crossings
and now where sun hits
a speeding windscreen
something strikes *the eye*
or is it the gilded pinnacle
of *that dominating dome*
it exists only to be looked
at denying the use it is
put to though it is
good to have a *roof* over
something or to love all
beings without exception
a *fishhook* may also be
of use after the assault
Philomel could not speak
a word her story
woven in coloured thread

3

Wake: a line of foam that
shoots out from the
back of a yellow speed-boat
why now think of the beaten
gong's *mottled surface* those
dimpling shifts of tone as
light makes *russet brandy
toffee rust* and *sand*
play in the air when some
kind of thatching is
perhaps more what is
needed with an opening
to the air indeed then a fire
might be made its *glow*
rising to the base of *an
inverted pyramid* that
bows in grace before a storm
tell Go Huan that the robe the
goddess wears has no seams

4

   hazard lights that blink on
a truck parked   on the
    far   bank of the river
rapid   information   *dazzles*
underneath our feet no need
to *fence* ourselves   apart
from these   *branching*
connections   of   naked
metal that   *articulate* a
particular   integration
of beauty   and use
    solitariness
takes on a *religious* character
as   in the shaping of clay
also the operation of the lathe
is work   for the *destroyer*
so quietly you unpick
at   night   the   pattern
    made the day before

5

Pale birch trees   tall and bare
   stretch   up to us   as if
we called for a higher thought
wealth moving through   the
city's vaults   invisible in
messages bouncing through
the air   *Hatton Garden craft*
part   remembered dispatched
as cyclists *thread*   the streets
as if   hunting some *animal*
aiming to stretch its skin
making some kind   of shelter
Gods   Men   Demons
the whole *vegetable* world
announce none is equal to
the sky   and   the stars
and the *brown eagle*   as well
she spins she draws lots while
the other turns her back away

6

A crane at an angle
to the horizon's broad stroke
is offering a way out
the metal *weathers* so that
we see a copse in evening
light *nearly transparent* the
new leaves on high branches
and the *dark copper* of what's
fallen on the path below
or lift your head up to
a sky that stretches
as the *desert* unpeopled
or the deep below we
should gather reeds before
our world goes to pieces
braiding them into a *torus*
a crown for the head
of the woman who builds the
image that she cannot look at

Diving into *The Waves*

Why is he saying this?
There is birdsong in the wood.
This is the peace you have waited for.
I no longer trouble myself with meaning.
I customize timpani and look out on the moon.
Light comes; light goes; we make light-bulbs you say.
The glassware is taken from the dishwasher and settled on shelves.
They are celebrating some remark about a country house.
A parrot has given the visitors occasion to smile.
There he is, waving his arms at the playpen.
'The case study blocks up the hall.'
The rhythm moves the room.
I say to come.
My opinion is to give.
The statue can be made to talk.
They are celebrating the beat generation.
I am not called upon to gladden my opponent.
There he is, waving his arms at the end of the platform.
The hinge of the world goes golden yet I am not called upon.
She walks towards him, wondering who'll be the first to smile.
In the high season unconsidered words continue to hurt.
A million hands stitch, raise hods with bricks.
The lights come into this room again.
He is there too.
Why is he saying this?
I let the million hands stitch.
A piano has been placed to suggest spontaneity.
There is a history of these meetings, statues, a cinematography.
He wheels his case past strangers, as information is updated.
The golfball was the root of his comeuppance.
Its flight is following the curve of the bay.

The leaves fly because he has passed.
A life comes and he leaves it open.
Our lake is heaving with fish.
There is no-one behind me.
It blocks up the way.
Headlines are intrusive.
Almost all high gates are iron.
Our long held hopes are frayed.
The kitchen door opens and shuts.
He leaves it open for others to enter.
I leave to others the voice of conviction.
The long afternoon of the service and the served.
Building is moving skyward, heading along the arms of cranes.
The soles of the waitress's shoes sound on the wooden floor.
The state continues to comment on the budget.
Some will never come into this room again.
Who else feels stone stairs ache?
The sideways glance.
I too feel the rhythm of Ebbw Vale.
The lightning conductor is worn out.
I am not called upon to give my opinion.
The digitized voice announces unplanned malfunctions.
They are meeting face-to-face in a patisserie next to the Hilton.
So we begin our return to the daily concerns of living.
In the window behind them is continual movement.
But not here, the rag-trade is outsourced east.
Life, life, I told you we have a life.
Is this the voice of possession?
The pope has few clients.
A chief problem is ash.
Hush now.

Palette

What faces us is an immeasurable
and shifting variation of blue that
Pantone was never prepared for.

Azure and cerulean are old sound
pictures, dictionary stand-ins for
the play of light on vapour in front.

You thought the spring sand singular
almost monumental until you kicked
against its granular particularity.

While particles collide or recombine,
notice the damp blue-black streaks
among the mustard on the water's edge.

Room

It seems you've spent significant time
in this room, or one like it,
or in that state of mind where will
recedes and consciousness occupies
itself with calculations,
fragments of tune, anything to
avoid attending to what is
present in the moment. And then

a field of action may emerge
with shouts from the crowd, sudden
movement, surprising poise and grace,
and subsequent analysis
accompanied by clips of film.
It will seem inevitable
that all slides back to words and
that presence slides from each

as each word is repeated
until the eye attends to
details of ceiling and cornice,
the ear to shifting of bodies
in seats, the body to its breath,
and you relax your need to find
a pattern in any of this,
as your name is called.

Andalucía

Though the street leads down
to the old power source

and there's an amiable air
to a tabernacle that's far

from any telling, I do not home
there as the sparrow to her nest.

Shadow draws a line across the street.
A cypress pierces the sky.

A vine climbs over the balcony
as the alley tightens its grip.

The dancer's weight moves to his toes.
Rose petals shine like beads

Words hidden behind panels
shine in the dust-clothed light.

Yellow

It's different from the yolk of an egg or
the flash of colour on a small bird's chest
or municipal daffodils drooping
in a side-street where an ambulance waits.

The flash of colour on a small bird's chest
passes in an instant. You concentrate,
in a side-street where an ambulance waits,
to hold it on the retina. The thought

passes in an instant. You concentrate
on other things: the paper, the novel,
to hold it on the retina. The thought
you had before this thought, before you looked

on other things. The paper the novel
is printed on is yellow, like an idea
you had before this thought, before you looked
across the street, where the sign the warning

is written on is yellow, like an idea
or municipal daffodils drooping
across the street, where the sign, the warning
is different from the yolk of an egg or…

The remixes

Fragments from the triple-gorge

(Sappho/Du Fu)

1

This onslaught of blossoms won't last.
There and my thoughts of there run away.

Bitten by a bramble bush I untangle
the knotted hair of your wounded song.

Such beautiful gifts. Green-kingfisher cliffs.
Skin lined already. More white hair than black.

The clear sounding lute welcomes my failures.
Look away. It is all a single grief.

The dancers are lighter on their feet than fawns.
Dawn, arms full of roses, sits on battered waves.
The haze lightens then goes dark. Imagining
       an end to struggle.

2

What shame should there be desiring what's beautiful,
loving delicate things, or striving for good?
Half the mountain is still perfumed with spring and
      the scent lasts past noon.

A sick man propped in bed, throat dry with coughing,
looks long at a basket of apricot, ripe pear and plum.

The glittery sandal-straps that come from Sardis,
the movement of light on a loved face, these memories.

Calligraphy like pine needles scattered on silk
showing wild seas and winding mountain ranges.

You bite at your own soul longing for the past
and reaching out to the far ends of thought.

Irises on Whittlesey Mere

(Clare/Mallarmé)

I'm sure of that.
Two of us were walking
facing out the landscape's many charms
comparing them to ours.

Certainty starts
to tremble though, when what
both of us remember in our bones –
this noon brilliance,

the lake island,
a hundred flags waving
– stays unnamed in summer's golden roll-call.
Companion, let's insist

an untrodden place
deep inside the marsh
hides the rumoured nest that birds choose to make
in iris-hidden hush;

rank tufts of sedge
or a willow tree's roots
swell some rising saturated earth to edge
above unruly shoots;

a long sharp bill
shaped like a planing tool
digs deep into the marshland's little hill
to pull out worms for food.

Yes, on an isle
seen with our actual eyes,
wings folding pitched a muted quaking camp
blanketed by flowers.

Each unfolded
petal spread out broadly,
so immense we had no words; a border
of light trimmed each flower.

Exaltation
filled my body and mind.
More wisely, you smiled with pleasure at this
work of vegetation,

noting the stalks'
unwonted growth with calm.
If man nor boy nor stock has found this spot
my wonder is a lie;

the water fowl
circle a swamp that's drained.
Instead of ampleness, we've come upon a
trickling, weeping channel.

Or, off the map,
we can ignore the world's ways
hearing snipe call across the still water
hidden by a floral veil.

Forest Burial

(Clare/Mallarmé)

Near here the ringdove coos, live wings folded.
Its otherworldly keening begins to shade
the future's glitter, that flickering light
that seemed to silver the sombre parade.

The wood's leafy order was shaken
by a startling haste of clapping wings.
You doubled down the corner of the page
you hadn't read, to keep in mind such things.

You scan the airy ups and downs of flight
and seek fresh patterns in the circling ring
and trace across the parti-coloured skies,
illluminations in the winter light.

Furious since the cold wind let it roll,
a dark rock tumbles. Our well-meaning hands
feel for a sign that it follows human plans
as if its crust of lichen were a soul.

Response to a Request

                You asked
             Catullus for a poem
               hoping, I suppose
                for something
                    FRUITY
                 with the SLAP
              of FLESH and TICKLE of
               his wit. He disappoints.
               His mind is with that
               round-faced friend who
               disappeared last summer,
               leaving only his laughing
                    voice behind.
                  Well… since
                you asked, here's a
             translation, from a long-dead
           poet. Think of it as like that apple
           the lover picked and gave to the girl
           who hid it under her dress, the cold
           fruit skin like a secret kiss against her
           skin. Think of the blush on the girl's face
         as   hearing her mother at the door,   she
       stood up in a guilty rush
                              letting the fruit fall
                         rolling slowly
                                    along the wooden floor

Catullus, Carmina LXV i.m. M G-R

At the Emperor's Court

(Sir Philip Sidney *An Apology for Poetry*)

Mine ears were exercised with slow payment.
Masters of war and speedy goers proceeded.
He persuaded me that self-love is better than
my unelected vocation. Bear with me. I make a
pitiful defence. Will they now play the hedgehog?
Stony people beautify our mother tongue. High
flying liberty did seem to have some force in it.

His telling of hills leaping showeth himself a
passionate lover. He goeth hand in hand with
Nature ranging within the zodiac of his own wit.
Let grammarians dispute delight. The final end
is made worse by clayey lodgings, old mouse-
eaten records built on the foundation of hearsay.
I found my heart moved more with a trumpet.

I would thou couldst as well defend thyself as thou
offend others. It is a chain shot against learning,
making a school-art of divine delightfulness. Plato
was made a slave with like cavillation. Idle England
can scarce endure the pain of a pen. Already the
triflingness is much too much enlarged. If you cannot
hear the planet-like music, then be rhymed to death.

Legend

All stories have some truth at heart, she said
thinking of the story told in the church
across the way from the pub in that far
village they'd reached across headlands, shaky
cliff paths, stone stiles and easy-giving mud.
The small black-painted chair with a sylkie
carved along one side inspired the tale of
Matthew the boy whose treble held the breath

of Sunday folk and even caught the ear
of the fish-tailed girl from the cove below
who keened along with him until he found
her hiding place and swam with her into
the open sea.   *What sort of truth is that?*
It is the heart's truth that such stories have.

An Old Tale
after Ovid

The wonder of the thing.

Father and son go door-to-door searching shelter.
It's said they can give and take away the forms of things.
Now, by a low wall, an oak and a lime tree stand side by side.
Loons and coots dive for scraps above the sunken village.

Equal in love and in the tasks they undertook
the couple faced their life and called it happiness,
in a home roofed with marsh reeds and stems.

And took strangers into the hearth of their heart's home
as thousands wouldn't.

They countered the slope of the table with a wedge
and served the neck-meat stew with greens.

The guard-goose honked at the smell of magic.
The visitors rushed them up the mountainside.

An arrow-shot below the top, they turned to look down
holding onto their sticks in shock as the village sank.

Traffiques and Discoveries

'the prose epic of our modern English nation'
— J A Froude

'This was a venture, sir, that Jacob served for;
A thing not in his power to bring to pass,
But sway'd and fashion'd by the hand of heaven.'
— *The Merchant of Venice*

Navigations, Voyages, Traffiques and Discoveries of the English Nation in Africa is the eleventh volume, in its 1889 edition, of the monumental work edited by Richard Hakluyt. Richard Hakluyt, Scholar of Christ Church Oxford, Prebendary of Bristol Cathedral, friend of Sidney and Raleigh, is not to be confused with his cousin, Richard Hakluyt, member of Middle Temple and friend of the spymaster Walsingham and the magician John Dee. The volume opens with accounts of a voyage undertaken in 1389 by 'Henry Earl of Derby, after Duke of Hereford and lastly Henry the fourth King of England to Tunis in Barbary'.

Polidore Virgill explains that Charles VI of France, at the bidding of the Genoese, decided to 'wage war against the Moors', a late Crusade aimed in part to combat piracy in the Mediterranean. He continues 'Likewise Richard the second, King of England, sent Henry the Earl of Derby unto the same warfare'. Yet it was not Henry Earl of Derby, the Bolingbroke we know from Shakespeare's history plays, who went on the expedition but his illegitimate half-brother, John Beaufort Earl of Somerset. So this record of the earliest English involvement with Africa provides an inaccurate account of an ignoble venture.

I am reading Hakluyt in a microfilm copy from the University of Alberta, online via *archive.org*. Navigating is a more appropriate term perhaps for this scrolling through indexes and pages of text; and navigation is at the heart of the matter: details of coastline, currents and climate; island resting places with their unfamiliar crops, ships encountered from other lands friendly or hostile. Wading through this accumulation of information the reader, or scroller, comes suddenly (and shockingly) on passages rich in vocabulary and rhetoric: Elizabethan prose, exotic in its way as tropical flora, bringing discoveries of cold barbarity driven by profit.

The first voyage to Guinea and Benin departed from Portsmouth in 1553 with two captains: Anthonie Anes Pinteado, an experienced Portuguese navigator, and Thomas Wyndham, Vice-Admiral. Martin Frobisher was a crew-member and might well be the author of the anonymous account Hakluyt collects. This narrative contrasts Pinteado 'a wise discreet, and sober man' with Wyndham, an 'unequal companion with virtues few or none adorned'. Wyndham 'showing a muster of the tragical parts he had conceived in his brain' soon takes sole command 'most shamefully abusing Pinteado: *whoreson Jew I will cut off his ears and nail them to the mast.*'

In Benin, Pinteado along with 'certain of the merchants' had an audience with the Oba, whose 'gentleness grew'. A trade of fourscore tons of pepper was negotiated. Waiting thirty days for this to be loaded 'our men having no rule of themselves' – they drank Palm wine and ran continually into the water in extreme heat – 'were brought into swellings and agues, which caused them to die 4 or 5 in a day'. Wyndham commanded the merchants to come away forthwith, threatening to leave them behind. 'Raging he broke up Pinteado's cabin, and in the mean time falling sick, himself died.'

Pinteado desired to fetch the rest of the merchants that were left at the Oba's court, but all was in vain. Other officers 'did spit in his face', saying he had been brought there to kill them, some drawing their swords. He was 'thrust among the boys, glad to find favour at the cook's hand'. 'He died for very pensiveness that stroke him to the heart. One worthy to serve any prince, and most vilely used (for what can be well ministered in a commonwealth where inequality will rule with tyranny)'. 'Of sevenscore men came home to Plymouth scarcely forty'.

The following year's bargaining was hindered by memories of the previous encounter, particularly the theft of a 'muske cat'. 'The fame of their misusage so prevented them that the people would bring no wares. They are very wary people in their bargaining. They that have to do with them must use them gently.' The merchants had to restore the cat or pay their price. Overall the voyage was profitable: four hundred 'and odde' pounds in weight of twenty-two carat gold, thirty-six butts of grain, and two hundred and fifty Elephant's teeth, some of nine spans in length. A sizeable graveyard.

William Towson gives an account of voyages to Guinea in 1555 and 1556. He writes, 'I observed some of their words of speech, which I thought good here to set down.' As an aid to future travellers, he notes *besow bezow* as a salutation, *mangete* and *crocow* as 'grains' and 'hens', *veede* as a verb 'to empty', demands for a knife or for bread as *begge sarke* and *begge come*, and two more striking phrases: *borke* – 'hold your peace'; *contreckeye* 'you lie'. It would seem from this sample of vocabulary that these first English visitors were already gaining a reputation.

'There came a young fellow which could speak a little Portuguese. I sold him thirty nine basins and two white saucers, for three ounces of gold. He told us the Portugals were bad men, and they made them slaves. This fellow demanded, why we had not brought their men, which the last year we took away. Five taken away by Englishmen. We answered him, that they were well used, and were kept in England till they could speak the language, and then they should be brought again to help Englishmen in this country. He spake no more of that matter.'

'Commodities and wares most desired in Guinea betwixt Sierra Leona and the furthest place of the Mina coast: Bracelets of brass, and some of lead. Basins of divers sorts. Pots of coarse tin. Wedges of iron. Some blue coral. Horse tails. Linen cloth principally. Kettles of Dutch-land with brass handles. Great brass basins, such as in Flanders they set upon their cupboards. Lavers, such as be for water. Chests of rowan of low price. Gowns, cloaks, hats, red caps, Spanish blankets, axe heads, hammers, slight bells, gloves of a low price, leather bags, and what other trifles you will.'

In Bristol, in 1961, my last year of primary school, I remember seeing the phrase 'Merchant Venturers' chalked on a blackboard. I'd read in *Look and Learn* about Da Gama inching his way from horizon to horizon to the Equator, past the cape of Good Hope, on to the Spice Islands. I'd read about Magellan and Drake's circumnavigations. The Cabots had sailed from here; and here I learned the phrase 'triangular trade'. Cheap manufactured goods sent from Bristol to the West African coast; then the dreadful cargo across the middle passage; from there raw materials to Liverpool for further manufacture.

William Towson's second voyage (in 1556) includes another visit to Benin, a town 'by the estimation of our men, as big in circuit as London'. He also writes of Africans being 'brought home' to Guinea: 'the people were very glad of our Negroes, specially one of their brothers wives, and one of their aunts, which received them with much joy'. The possessive 'our Negroes' seems significant. Quite soon they are given European names. George, our Negro'. 'George and Binny came to us, and brought with them two pound of golde'. Between the lines of his account we witness something beginning.

Benin remained free of colonization until the 1890s. The Oba's imposition of customs duties on palm oil and ivory rankled British traders. Since the 1860s, the orientalist Richard Burton and others had waged a propaganda campaign against the 'barbarity' of the kingdom with the aim of making it British. Following the ambush of an undercover invasion, a 'punitive expedition' was sent to Benin in 1897 to be financed by the sale of looted art objects. Benin City was razed to the ground; its entire population massacred. Accounts of human sacrifice discovered during the attack were used to justify its destruction.

Much of the eleventh volume is concerned with other issues than Africa. A meeting with a Portuguese traveller who had been a prisoner in China leads to a lengthy account of what is to be found further East: customs, topography, political organisation. 'The regional categories created by Hakluyt are interesting when they *don't* track physical geography. A series of trading voyages with West Africa can be found in the second half of Volume 2. Hakluyt's third volume, devoted to the Americas, includes very significant information: for instance, John Hawkins' attempts at imitating the Spanish trade in Africans'.

(Source: Hakluyt Society)

In a succinct account of a 1562 voyage, we find John Hawkins hearing 'that Negroes were very good merchandise in Hispaniola, and that store of Negroes might easily be had upon the coast of Guinea'. He received enthusiastic backing for a trial voyage from 'liberal contributors and adventurers' in England. In Sierra Leone he 'got into his possession, partly by the sword, and partly by other means, to the number of 300 Negroes... besides other merchandises'. With 'prosperous success and much gain to himself and the aforesaid adventurers' Hawkins returned home in 1563 from Hispaniola via the Islands of Cacos.

So to the account of John Hawkins's voyage of 1564, which takes us gently from Plymouth to Madeira and Tenerife, *fortunate isles* of antiquity 'for sugar, sweets, raisins of the sun... abundance', and digresses lengthily on the nature of the camel whose 'nature is to engender backwards contrary to other beasts'. Less space is given when the ships (the *Tiger* and the *Jesus* of Lubeck) reach the Callowasa, a river in Gambia where Hawkins (who'll be knighted at sea by the Queen at the time of the Armada) 'dispatched his business, and so returned with two caravels, laden with negroes'.

This commerce with Portuguese traders inspired Hawkins to go further. Once 'advertised... of a town' with 'a great quantity of gold', and 'not above forty men and an hundred women and children', he planned an attack 'so that he might get an hundred slaves'. That word uttered, the indifference to common humanity becomes plain. Hawkins's men, scattered through the town in search of gold, were trapped by returning Africans. The sailors retreated. Seven of them were killed; '27 hurt'. The captain 'in a singular wise manner carried himself, with countenance very cheerful outwardly, having gotten by our going ten negroes'.

Visiting the central area of Bristol in the 1960s, I was aware of the figure of Edmund Burke, arm raised as if hailing a taxi, which stood near the city's main department store and its bus station. Yet, though I knew his surname from the private schools in the city and the concert hall where I'd seen the Rolling Stones and the Incredible String Band, I'd never seen the brooding index of Edward Colston nearby, arms folded eyes downcast, until its immersion into the harbour last June and its temporary replacement with Marc Quinn's triumphant, resolute study of Jen Reid.

Hakluyt's accounts are sketchy about the fate of Hawkins's captives in the Americas, focussing on the bargaining skills of the 'worshipful and valiant knight'. In what became Venezuela, he attempted a sale of 'certain lean and sick negroes', but was faced with delays in issuing a trading licence and high customs duties. Hawkins marched on the town with a hundred men 'well armed with bows, arrows, arquebuses and pikes' and trade at a lower customs rate was agreed. In a third 'troublesome' voyage the opposition to trade was more violent and Hawkins returned unsuccessful to Mounts Bay, Cornwall in 1568.

Accounts of capture and enslavement from those who were trafficked only appear later in the eighteenth century. Among these Olaudah Equiano's *Interesting Narrative* is perhaps the best known. Equiano writes of being 'handled, and tossed up to see if I were sound' and of seeing 'a multitude of black people... chained together'. 'On my refusing to eat, one of them held me fast by the hands... and tied my feet, while the other flogged me severely'. 'I had never experienced among any people such instances of brutal cruelty... not only shewn towards us blacks, but to the whites themselves'.

Hawkins's discovery, in the face of an embargo backed by Spanish ordinance, that human trafficking was unprofitable brought English interest in the trade to a close until the next century. In 1569 an English court heard the judgement that 'England was too pure an air for a slave to breathe in'; a sudden lurch to the moral high ground that would last for a generation or two. Hakluyt's work, with its mission to develop English settlement in North America, laid the ground for its gradual resumption. African slavery was introduced to Jamestown in 1619 and to Barbados in the 1640s.

Hakluyt was a scholar and archivist, a churchman and a propagandist for global expansion. He travelled little outside his home country, though as a young man had hoped to be taken on as a ship's chaplain on expeditions in the North Atlantic. A century later, Colston was a large investor in the Royal African Company, becoming its deputy governor at a time when the trafficking of enslaved people was its second most profitable venture, then retiring to philanthropy. The profiteer and the political lobbyist were insulated from the violence and criminality their work enabled elsewhere. It was business as usual.

Equiano was baptised in St Margaret's church, Westminster, taking the name Gustavus Vassa. This is the church where Milton was married. Walter Raleigh is buried near the altar. A window commemorates William Caxton, who was also buried here. The church, which neighbours Westminster Abbey, is in a corner of Parliament Square which is home to statues of Peel and Disraeli, Lincoln and Gandhi, Churchill and Mandela, and latterly Gillian Wearing's sculpture of Millicent Fawcett. Equiano is memorialised in the church of his baptism with a small oval plaque displaying a sixteen word inscription in a modern typeface, unveiled in 2009.

2020 Visions

Taking Notice

Not to let it pass, but to enter
the ongoing spiral of other lives,
to escape the pull of the star's core,
to drift from the spinning surface
like ions and electrons arriving
in the choral brilliance of terminal
shock.
        So we are pulled to the hand
reaching from the darkness of the hold,
the arm arched for the next rung,
the arm nesting a child. And to
plot this attention, geometry is
called for, a grid to bring the eye
into focus. The way he applies
razor and comb to follow a line
or curve he has in mind.

                          That scruple.

Because we are not here for ever,
we choose this moment to do what
can be done and keep what will be
to be uncovered later: a landscape
etched from rock and ice, whose
stern beauty we can put to one side,
letting the ear curl around the
sound of a string trio aspiring to
the low purring of a favoured cat.

Not everything must be attended to.
The mind decides at times to
untie the thread, to walk away.

Dublin, 31.1.20

In a new city, the eye is drawn
to sculpture: these figures on pillars,
plinths, facades. Nation-building statesmen,
sages, soldiers and abstract virtues stand
or stretch themselves, some caught in thought,
one ready to address oncoming
crowds, or traffic – unaware a bird
preens its feathers perching on his head.

I'm more at home with a small study
of marguerites on a mantelpiece.
Unnecessary, intimate art
holds the eye steady as we unpick
the secret bargain of metaphors.

Likeness assumes difference.
The link to what's known
distracts us from what's strange.
Or difference masks likeness.
Groups gather on either side of the raft
to raise their flags, better to know
an enemy than the direction home.

Breaking Away

Montale's young man walks alongside
a rough stone wall topped with broken glass.
The fields on his side are green enough.

So why the desire to leap across?
Why, on the other side, would he feel
the same – the landscape he left behind

performing its own magnetism?
Should he seek shelter where the hill's slope
works against him, or on the level

ground where he can see water rising?
(Two children run in a ring seeking
the safe space they can claim in the game.)

He has climbed to a clearing of sorts,
dazed to learn how far he has travelled,
the pinnacle still covered by cloud.

In the distance birds buckle and dive.
(His fingers tighten their grip on the
self-help guide; his frown seems to deepen.)

The challenge may be to move from the
self-portrait to the landscape, to the
detail of what grows between grasses,

to what goes crawling there, making its
difference known, standing apart from
the rest in excitement or despair.

Naming the Wind

Finding no self to confront the world,
he crafts a structure so intricate he
feels the pain that he once faked.
He's out-of-place as an orange-tree
to Keats. This potted one sits outside
a Flask Walk shop, in February,
before the snowdrops start to
push their way above the earth.

Having lost an argument, a new torment
is to hear the same words rehearsed,
as if by repetition they could persuade.
It takes a fierce wind with an appointed
name to shift our vision. Meanwhile,
we scrutinise our plans to make, remake,
extend or undermine. Or we stand above
the dusk-shaded city and try to guess
names of places from their shadow selves.

The Maze

As when, in a laboratory,
one rat chooses his best path and sticks
to it, so I had thought I knew the

best cut-throughs. Yet you found a passage
that made the streets unfamiliar,
just as I began my journey out.

And now we walk by the pool
of the river watching seabirds dive
and circle, indifferent to how they
are seen, and to our admiration.

'Look how far I've climbed!' cries
the child, running to the end. Others
are sitting propped against walls, a placard
in their lap to explain their stories.

Comrades

How we are represented is now
an issue. The placard-holders are
gathered in the square. It's not enough
to be *like* us; it should be *of* us, a shining
forth of who we are. It should belong
to us and we to it, as an item placed
in storage – in our lives, but hidden.
We pay for the knowledge, knowing
it's elsewhere.
                     Are you with me?
I don't need to ask. We both stopped
in our steps for the street-singer's voice,
the words in which she'd placed
whatever love she'd known, and all that
she knew of what was taken from her.

Meanwhile we talk across tables
missing the point of the last remark,
hoping it's our words stay in the
mind of the first to leave.

Or the last,
since all leave in the end. And walk
home through streets that we recall,
though we do not call them *ours*.

Distractions

Ali Smith's novel *Spring* is out in paperback.

While you wash your hands, try to recall
the detail of your mother's story
about – what was it? – a country place,
a word like 'arboretum' suggests itself.

Heath Robinson imagined flat-
dwellers welcoming the spring
with eurythmics on their balconies,
led by an instructress in a balloon.
The pleasures of vertical living.
High-rise access to the open air!

Modernity has stayed with us a while,
bar empty shelves for paper goods
and trolleys filled with bottled water.

Sometimes excess is tolerable.
Sometimes we plump for greater restraint
planning for a single shrub, perhaps,
circled by a covering of slate.

The trees are out though,
persistent in their return.
As we drive slowly through the suburb
magnolia starts to bloom. Gilt-rimmed
vessels lifted to a clearing sky.

Circles

In Dante's long catalogue of souls,
some are judged, some pitied, some revered.
It's hard to make such sharp distinctions
circling the supermarket aisles.

We keep our distance advisedly,
moving briskly among the half-filled shelves,
looking intently to our needs
while others look to theirs, and shop-workers
weigh extra shifts against extra risks.

Climbing up our nearby hill,
there's time to pause and note how
beyond the lines of roofs, hills rise up
behind the hills. Our phoned exchanges
orbit the mind as days expand.

Our new excursions are briefer,
nearer home. There's time to notice
daily changes beyond statistics:
a different flower in that window,
blossom now falling from the trees.

Llandudno

Neither charedi nor chapel people are disturbed by the new arrivals. There have been stories of such a descent from the heights for decades. From Kashmir to Windsor to this limestone head named for a sea-monster, they have nuzzled and munched their way into the life of the town with its Punch and Judy, its pier stalls selling rockabilly CDs, its seafront benches facing North.

But with streets largely empty, traffic rare, and seabirds calling as they range more widely searching for nourishment, there's something uncanny about the ease of these horned nibblers rubbing their white coats against privet hedges.

1/4/20

Roses

This seems to be the day roses,
all along the streets we walk in,
decide to draw attention to
themselves – stiffening, growing
more definite in their colours.

And even the spent silver nitrous
oxide capsules, twinkling in the sun's
glint under the tree near the bus stop,
start to look like evidence of
someone's reckless grasp at joy.

On such days some, their faces set
in considered expressions, utter
rehearsed commands, thrilled beyond
thought by the exercise of power.

Back from Leave

Finding out the ectoplasmic complicates things,
and perhaps castles pass the parcel – such are
the consequences of putting your mind to work

filling the blanks of a grid. Those permitted
not to work fill time like filling a trench
with sand or counting peas in a bowl and

counting again to check the count. A kind
of rhythm becomes established in which
there is soon time for improvisation or

purposeful research into the distinctions
between trees. And then the bugle's plangent,
persistent tone sounds a return to action.

Children chatting outside school gates assert
their presence at a muted pitch. Dates are
ringed on calendars. And when directives come

– mumbled, ambiguous – we look askance.
Was it always like this? It seems it was.

Looking Westward

(A Golden Shovel for Derek Mahon)

Because I thought a melancholy horn played in the
distance, I looked towards the low-lying sun
on the construction site. New building rises
somewhere each week. That some have faith in
a future is comforting. If some act of spite
shifts your mood, makes you afraid of
what's coming, it's good to know everything,
even that troubling sound, is subject to change and
fast-flowing water may soon ride over the
rocks to fill the pool. Yes, winter isn't far
away but, even in our guarded times, cities
bring us face to face with other lives. Many are
gathered in open spaces taking in what's beautiful
in the passing of the growing year and
looking back at the sun – still low, yet bright.

The Pear Tree

after Giacomo da Lentini

How wonderful it is
that this tightens its hold
dragging me back at all hours,
like an artist whose mind
is stuck in one place
with the old image again,
all powers focussed
as if at the start
on a form held in the heart.

It seems I've taken you to heart
as if the real thing
not the copy that I've made.
I feel such shame
that I just look at you,
the light catching your form
on the other side of the canal,
like a believer
confiding in an icon.

There's dancing

in Philadelphia PA
New York City too
don't forget DC

dancing in the Plaza
the Avenue the Square

and here in the park
though it's cold
there's dancing

six-year old twins
a boy and a girl
dance for themselves
while their parents
sit back on the grass

there's dancing
in the November sun

and words are dancing
between the two men
quietly discussing
a retreat from addiction

the halloumi
in my takeaway lunch
is squealing with delight

the pigeons
pivoting in formation
take part in the silent disco

a sullen man
sits in a golfcart
wearing a silly hat

he is not dancing

squirrels in gardens
who hang upside down
while raiding birdfeeders
are dancing

the dancers wear masks
saying VOTE or HOPE

inside the masks
they are smiling

or they are singing songs
about the cities
they love

they will dance into the night
and tomorrow
there will be work to be done

7.11.20

The Mysteries

While I would wish to work
                from axiomatic first principles
to logically certain conclusions
                it is still unclear to me
whether it was an owl I heard
                or a late pigeon cooing.

A step into the woods
                I had forgotten were there
and high in the trees
                a confusion of signals
the darkening sky
                the scattered birds calling.

Syllogistic reasoning
                applied to disambiguated
definitions can take us
                only some of the way
as we follow an arbitrary path
                between assertive pines.

When the runner passing by
                breathes out
the same reiterated phrase
                I need to break the cycle
I'm taken by an image
                of wire-cutters and a chain.

Does the breeze lead us on
                to a promise of water
or are we following a memory
                dream has transformed
into something between
                seduction and theft?

Whatever I flinch from
               in a too-loud voice
or a too-crowded room
               leaves
settled opinion
               unchallenged, serene.

I can see the train's
               headlights entering
the bend of the track
               and the sunset
spilling out along
               the lower sky.

Circumstances favour decisive
               statements of purpose
while I hesitate to confirm
               whether I will in fact
or whether I shall indeed
               express a conclusion.

Mornington Crescent

Looking at the picture, you start to understand how
ghost presences can result from material decay.
That smudge of grey disturbing the stubborn white
modernity of the art-deco frontage – is someone

standing there taking the scene in? The Carreras
factory, then Greater London House. Will it soon
be luxury flats? This is the view from below Sickert's
balcony, but I'm thinking about Auerbach's daily

return to scrape the canvas and start again, to go
out in the street and imagine the scene as vertical
or angled lines, patches of colour overlaid and
mounted on each other, just as what is seen is

built over what we remember but cannot
obliterate it. Rather what was there persists:
the communal garden, some hidden brook
perhaps heard murmuring beneath your feet.

Defrosting

In those days, when refrigerators' inner walls iced up and a furry kind of snow fringed the frozen food compartment not unlike icing inside and out, then it would make sense to leave the door wide open and listen out for the creaking noise as shapes of ice broke off.

Sometimes, we would help it on its way by hacking with a knife – though this was not thought right behaviour. The food would wait in patience on a nearby table, while a plastic bowl was in readiness to catch the chill meltwater and its soft attendant crumbs of waste.

Sea-ice is melting at its fastest pace since the year of the consulship of Paulus. An aerial photograph off the coast of Russia shows a mass resembling a particularly lacy crêpe on a smooth surface of Mediterranean blue. Permafrost blushes as it begins to soften and shift.

These days refrigerators have been regulated to defrost themselves. If you leave the door open while restocking or taking a late-night snack an alarm rings. If you keep it open, the alarm will make a louder shriek as you stop to pluck another, air-freighted, piece of fruit.

Tomsk

The Museum of Political Repression is on Lenin Street.
We walk towards the station most days of the week.
Adam admired the sheen on the surface of the seat
and looked towards the sunshine for evidence of defeat.
Beyond the extension stood the remembered trees.
There is something partial in what each of us sees.

Each carries his machine. The hidden code beneath
is stored in the nation's silos. Experts agree
that legislation has its limits. We must steel
ourselves to new eruptions of candid grief.
The solution is saturated, appearing bright green
in the harsh new light. And just beyond our reach.

Flying out of Constantinople

I had a Skype call in the early hours from the Topkapi Palace. At first all I heard was some mumbling about the Fates. The face was kindly, with no trace of malice. Only as I stumbled nearer, did I realise this was Yeats.

From the kiosk he sat in I watched Black Sea tankers glide past the Golden Horn. He wore a loose yellow cape and a turban of soft cream. I was drawn to a voice that seemed antique before I was born. *I am a consultant to the sultan in the area of dream.*

Tell me then why my father has suddenly broken into a run. He is moving ahead of the pack. Why is no-one alarmed as he races towards the sun? Is this him now, breathing hard lying on his back?

It's enough to weaken your eyes, scrutinising the all-surrounding dome. 'Talk to me', he says. 'Bring me stories of home'.

Two Rivers Press has been publishing in and about Reading
since 1994. Founded by the artist Peter Hay (1951–2003),
the press continues to delight readers, local and further afield,
with its varied list of individually designed,
thought-provoking books.